The Night Watch

PROPHETIC TIME CLOCK REVEALED

ROY S. MILLS

xulon PRESS

The Night Watch
by Roy S. Mills

Printed in the United States of America

ISBN-13: 978-1-59467-601-7
ISBN-10: 1-594676-01-1

Unless otherwise indicated Bible quotations are taken from the King James Version

Brief Quotations: Wycliffe Bible Encyclopedia The Moody Press of Chicago copyright © 1975

Brief Quotations: The Illustrated Bible Dictionary. Inter-Varsity Press copyright © 1980

Brief Quotations: The Concise Oxford Dictionary. Oxford University Press © 1976

www.xulonpress.com

DEDICATION

This book, first and foremost is dedicated to God., Without His inspired revelation this book would not exist. This is more than a book or a concept, it is a now word, a pre-alarm warning from God. Though we cannot put our finger on the exact day or hour of His return, we shall know the season and prepare our hearts before Him. Ten virgins were called, only five were ready.

This book is also dedicated to my precious wife Kerri, and my four children, Paul, Angela, Adam and John. They sacrificed their home, family and their friends in Australia, to support our mission to America. I pray God will richly bless my wonderful wife Kerri for her personal sacrifice and dedication to the Kingdom of God.

Roy S. Mills

INTRODUCTION

THE NIGHT WATCH

PROPHETIC TIME CLOCK REVEALED

Scripture teaches us to be aware of the **times and the seasons,** and to watch continuously for the coming of the Lord. This book was written in the light of such inspiration.

The Hebrew Night Watch was eventually divided into **four watches,** or four time frames to guard the city against potential invasion.

Jesus said, *"If the good man of the house had known in what watch the thief would come, he would have watched, and would not have suffered his house to be broken up."* (Mt. 24:43) Jesus implies in this scripture, that those who believe and remain at His coming should know in what **watch** He would come.

This book is the revelation of The Night Watch, **four watches in the night.** In the eyes of God the world remains in spiritual darkness, due to the fall of Adam and the curse of sin.

The Night Watch resembles this darkness and reveals the master plan of God's salvation. This plan is revealed through **four time frames** of biblical history, designated for the redemption of mankind on Planet Earth. **Four denotes the number of the earth.**

Each time frame contains a period of **2000 years,** with a total period of **8000 years** to complete the cycle of God's plan of redemption. **Eight denotes the number of new beginnings and cleasing.**

This revelation portrays Jesus Christ as the dividing factor between two **4000 year** periods.

The introduction of Christ to the world literally split time into two separate eras, BC and AD.

This book confirms the voice of the prophets and the signs of the times. Each chapter demonstrates an incredible parallel concerning natural and spiritual events.

A complete biblical overview from beginning to end is displayed within The Night Watch.

The **Prophetic Time Clock** reveals that three watches have now been fulfilled. We are entering the fourth and final watch concerning God's plan of redemption. A far greater picture is now visible to the 20th century Church.

I pray you experience a fresh zeal and excitement for the Kingdom of God, as you discover for yourself, the revelation of The Night Watch.

Sincerely in Christ. **Roy S. Mills**

CONTENTS

Chapter: 1   **THE NIGHT WATCH** **13**

    Four Time Frames 13
    Four Is The Number Of The Earth 13
    A Thousand Years As One Day 15
    The Prophetic Time Clock 15

Chapter: 2   **THE EASTERN GATE** **17**

    The Gateway To Heaven 17
    Children Of The East 18
    Four Corners Of The Earth 19
    The Prophetic Compass 21
    Four Windows 23
    The Tabernacle 27
    The Holy of Holies 29

Chapter: 3   **THE HEBREW HARVESTS**...........................**31**

    God's Total Harvest Plan 31
    The Seasons And Their Time Frames 34
    The Olive Harvest 38
    The Prophetic Calendar.................................40

Chapter: 4   **THE HEBREW FEASTS** **43**

                Feast Representations..............................43
                New Beginnings.....................................45

Chapter: 5   **THE MENORAH**...............................**47**

                Seven Golden Candlesticks.....................47
                Seven Dispensations Or Church Ages 47
                Nine Candlestick Hanukah – Menorah................50
                Total Duration Of God's Redemptive Plan..........50
                Nine Months Of Pregnancy 54
                Nine Denotes Judgment And Divine
                Completeness 54
                Eight Days Of Extended Grace..............55
                Eight Days Of Purification.....................57
                Christ The Light Bearer 59
                Christ The Branch 59

Chapter: 6   **THE CROSS**.................................**61**

                Six Hours On The Cross 61
                Darkness At Midday Until 3pm 61
                The Ninth Hour 63

Chapter: 7   **THE TEMPLE** **67**

                God's True Dwelling Place 67
                A Spiritual Temple 67
                A Perfect Structure Is Now Visible........67
                The Temple Of Zion..............................69
                Solomon's Temple.................................71

Chapter: 8   **THE NINTH MONTH** 73

The Birth Canal.................................73
The Birth Of A Nation........................74
The Church In Travail.........................75
The Hidden Ones 75
The Womb Of Creation.......................75

Chapter: 9   **SATAN'S ABORTION PLAN**...............77

Spiritual Adultery..............................77
Satan's Judgment Foretold...................77
The Flood.......................................78
Corruption At Conception....................78
Sin Is A Terminal Disease 79
God's Remedy For Sin........................79
Only The Righteous Will See The Light of Day....79
Premature Abortion Of The World...........80
God Has Not Forsaken His Children 81
The Only Way Out 81

Chapter: 10   **THE NIGHT IS FAR SPENT** 83

The Midnight Hour 83
Darkness Shall Cover The Earth.............85
Spiritual Darkness.............................85
The Prince Of Darkness.......................85
Put On The Whole Armor Of God 86
Delivered From Darkness 87
Watching And Waiting 87
The Times And The Seasons..................88
God Has Not Appointed Us To Wrath 89
Love Not The World 90

Chapter: 11   **THE MORNING WATCH** **91**

The Final Chapter 91
The Forth Watch..91
The Bright And Morning Star 92
A Generation Of Passionate Believers...................92
The Gathering Dispensation 93
The Final Fulfillments...............................94

Chapter: 12   **THE END OF ALL THINGS** **97**

The End Of The World...............................97
Behold! He Makes All Things New 99

Chapter One

THE NIGHT WATCH
Part 1

FOUR TIME FRAMES

The Night Watch was divided into **four time frames** covering a twelve-hour period, from six in the evening until six in the morning. In other words **six o'clock represents the first hour of the night or day.**

The Night Watch is the revelation of **four prophetic time frames,** also called dispensations or church ages. **These four time frames display God's redemptive plan from beginning to end,** for all mankind. God is not bound by time, He has no beginning or ending. The earth is suspended between eternity past and eternity future. **Time was only instituted for man in his fallen state.** When God's redemptive plan ends time will be no more.

FOUR IS THE NUMBER OF THE EARTH

Four is the number of the earth. This is very significant to The Night Watch.

God created the earth in **four days,** we have **four seasons,** and scripture speaks of **four winds.** Certain scriptures divide the world into **four parts** and described them as the **four corners** or **four quarters of the earth.** (Is. 11:12) (Rev. 7:1-20:8)

See Diagram: **THE NIGHT WATCH - Four time frames.**

THE NIGHT WATCH - Four time frames.

The Night Watch is the revelation of **four time frames** of biblical history. **Four watches** in the night to complete the cycle of God's redemption for all mankind. **Four time frames** designated for God's total harvest plan. **Four denotes the number of the earth.**

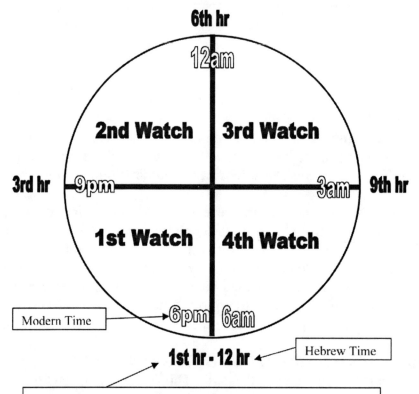

The Night Watch began at **6pm** and ended at **6am,** a **twelve-hour cycle.** The first hour of the Hebrew night or day began at six o'clock.
Important Note! **The first hour of the Night Watch is the starting point of the Prophetic Time Clock.**

Chapter One

THE NIGHT WATCH   Part 2

A THOUSAND YEARS AS ONE DAY

As God led me to study The Night Watch, the revelation of the four time frames became evident as I read scriptures such as Ps. 90:4 *For a thousand years in thy sight are but as yesterday when it is past, and as a __watch in the night.__* When this scripture linked a thousand years with reference to The Night Watch I was very excited. **Scripture also teaches us that prophetically a thousand years is as one day with the Lord.** (2 Pet. 3:8) With these scriptures in mind and the fact that the Hebrews divided the world into **four parts** and described them as the **four corners of the earth,** or the **four quarters of the earth,** (Is. 11:12) (Rev. 7:1-20:8) it became evident to me that God was revealing something deeper and more significant within The Night Watch.

THE PROPHETIC TIME CLOCK

The Prophetic Time Clock is the revelation of four time frames, each time frame represents a period of 2000 years, a total duration of 8000 years to fulfill all Bible prophesy.

Interesting to note numerically, that **number eight** is the number of new beginnings.

The following chapters of The Night Watch have an exciting significance and parallel, when placed upon the Prophetic Time Clock.

See Diagram: **THE PROPHETIC TIME CLOCK -** A thousand years as one day.

THE PROPHETIC TIME CLOCK - A Thousand Years as One Day

> The Bible speaks prophetically of **1000 years** as one day. The Prophetic Time Clock reveals a period of **8000 years** to complete the cycle of God's redemption. **Eight denotes the number of new beginnings and purification.**

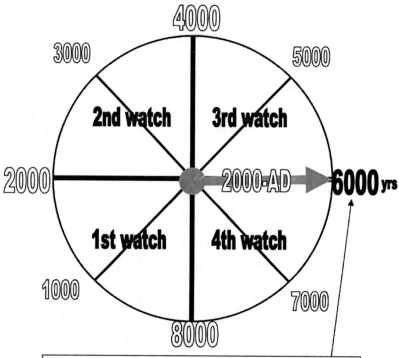

> **2000-AD** is parallel with approximately **6000 years** of biblical history. **Six denotes the number of man.**

THE EASTERN GATE
Part 1

THE GATEWAY TO HEAVEN

East is very significant at this hour in church history, considering the needle on the **Prophetic Time Clock** is now pointing directly east. East represents the opening or gateway to the presence of God.

I believe that the gateway is about to open for the resurrection and departure of the saints.

East represents a place of dawning and the rising of the sun, how fitting that Christ should come in the **fourth or morning watch,** the place of dawning and the rising of the sun. The year **2000 AD** parallels with the Eastern Gate on the Prophetic Time Clock. *"That's exciting"*

The Hebrew meaning for East is *Qedem* meaning **front or before** and *mizrah* meaning **the place of dawning** and the Greek word *anatole* meaning **the rising of the sun.**

➢ **East was the entrance to the Garden of Eden**
*So he drove out the man; and he placed **at the (east) of the Garden of Eden** Cherubim's and a flaming sword which turned every way to keep the way of the tree of life.* (Gen. 3:24)

➤ **East was the doorway to the Lords House**
*And the cherubim's lifted up their wings, and mounted up from the earth in my sight: when they went out, the wheels also were beside them, and **every one stood at the door of the (east gate) of the Lord's house;** and the glory of the God of Israel was over them above.* (Ezek. 10:19)

➤ **East was the entrance to the Tabernacle** (Num. 3:38)

The Hebrew and Semitic people looked to the **east** rather than the **north** for their point of direction. A person would face **east** making that direction his **front** or **before**. **West** would be to his back, **north** to his left, and **south** to his right.

CHILDREN OF THE EAST
Men of the east had a reputation of wealth and great wisdom. (1 Kings. 4:30) Job in his day was the greatest man of the east. (Job. 1:3) Wise men from the east came to worship Jesus led by the eastern star. Saying, *"Where is he that is born King of the Jews? For we have seen his star in the east and are come to worship him."* (Mat. 2:1,2)

I believe we are the **Children of the East;** we are the generation facing directly east on the **Prophetic Time Clock**. Hopefully we shall see the rising of the Son in our day. Christ will be manifest in us as the hope of glory. We are the generation awaiting the upward call and glorious manifestation of the sons of God. We are the children of double portion and the reapers of the final harvest. We are the glorious church under final instruction and preparation, the prophets desired to see our day and rejoiced.

_____

We are the Children of the East, Kings and Priests of the Most High God.

How fitting for the end time church to be assembled at the Eastern Gate.

Chapter Two

THE EASTERN GATE   Part 2

FOUR CORNERS OF THE EARTH

God is gathering His people from the four corners of the earth to the Eastern Gate, the matrix, *(meaning place of development)* the gateway to heaven. The Hebrews divided the world into four parts and described them as the four corners of the earth, or the four quarters of the earth. (Is. 11:12) (Rev. 7:1-20:8)

On the **Prophetic Time Clock** the Eastern Gate now parallels with **the final wheat harvest** and **the gathering of the grapes.** *(See Hebrew Harvest chapter)* God is sifting the wheat and tending His vine for the instant reaping of the earth. The Eastern Gate is the doorway to the **morning watch** and the **seventh millennium;** I believe the morning watch is dedicated to the Son of God, His glorious reign, and final judgment of the earth.

> *For as the lightning COMES OUT OF THE EAST, and shines even unto the west; so shall* also *the coming of the Son of Man be.* (Mat. 24:27)

See Diagram: **THE EASTERN GATE** - Four corners of the earth.

THE EASTERN GATE - Four Corners of the Earth.

When the Prophetic Time Clock is placed within the parameters of the **four corners of the earth**, the needle is pointing directly east at the year 2000-AD. East is used continually in scripture as a form of gateway or entrance to the presence of God. I believe the Church of Jesus Christ is now being assembled at the Eastern Gate.

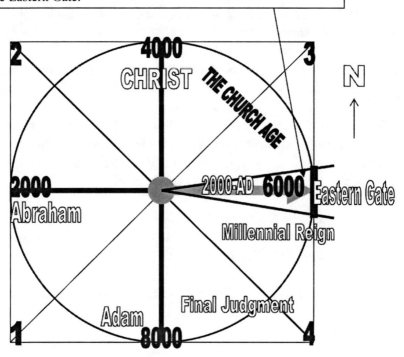

The year **2000-AD** and approximately **6000 years** of biblical history are now parallel with the Eastern Gate. The Eastern Gate is a type of **matrix, a form of birth canal** to the soon coming Kingdom of God. (Ref# ch.8)

Chapter Two

THE EASTERN GATE   Part 3

THE PROPHETIC COMPASS
The compass is very significant in The Night Watch revelation.

The needle on the "Prophetic Compass" is now pointing directly east!

This is a very exciting revelation for the Jews and the Gentiles, prophetically speaking.

East is the gateway to heaven (The place of dawning). The dawning of His glorious appearing is truly at hand. As the sunrises in the east, so shall **Christ, the Bright and Morning Star,** arise with healing in His wings.

There's a flickering on the horizon, the dawning of a new day. *"Get ready SAINTS!"*

See Diagram: **THE PROPHETIC COMPASS** - East is the gateway to heaven.

THE PROPHETIC COMPASS - East is the Gateway to Heaven.

When the **compass** is placed on the Prophetic Time Clock, the needle is pointing directly **east** at the year **2000-AD**. As previously mentioned east represents a doorway to the presence of God. The compass points and now declares the return of Jesus Christ.

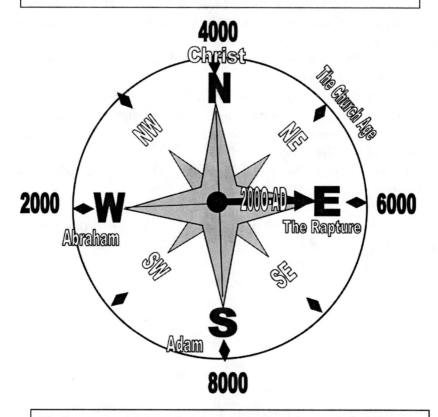

The **four main points on the compass** represent **four major windows** of heavenly interaction with mankind on the earth. 1. Adam and Creation: 2. Abraham and the Promises: 3. Christ and His Church: 4. The next major window of heavenly interaction will include:
- A great manifestation of God's power for the final harvest.
- The Resurrection and Rapture of the Church Age.
- The Final Judgment of the World Antichrist System.
- The establishment of the Kingdom of God on earth.

Chapter Two

THE EASTERN GATE   Part 4

FOUR WINDOWS North-South-East-West

THE FOUR MAJOR POINTS ON THE COMPASS REPRESENT FOUR MAJOR FOCUS POINTS OF HEAVENLY INTERACTION WITH GOD AND MANKIND.

1. **ADAM** - The conception of Mankind
2. **ABRAHAM** - The call of a Family
3. **CHRIST** - The birth of a Nation
4. **CHURCH** - The establishment of the Kingdom of God

WINDOW. No.1   ADAM - Southern Window
The first window of heavenly interaction with the earth is represented by God's creation and the conception of mankind.

WINDOW. No.2   ABRAHAM - Western Window
The second window of heavenly interaction is represented by the call of Abraham.

Abraham existed approximately **2000 years** before Christ. This time frame parallels perfectly with the western window, a major focus point on God's Prophetic Compass.

Abraham was a major representation of Christ, the church age, and the Kingdom of God.

Abraham represents God the Father, as he Abraham, offers his only son Isaac as a sacrifice.

Abraham's seed represents the inheritance of the world. (Rom. 4:13)

Abraham represents the living not the dead. (Mt. 22:32)

Abraham also represents:
Righteousness by faith in God: (Rom. 4:3)
The father of all that believe: (Rom. 4:11)

The father of many nations: (Rom. 4:18)
The father of promise: (Gal. 3:14-29)
The blessings of God: (Gal. 3:14)
The promise of the Holy Spirit by faith: (Gal. 3:14)

The first verse in the New Testament portrays Christ as the son of Abraham, according to his generations. (Mt. 1:1) Jesus took upon Himself the seed of Abraham. (Heb. 2:16)

Jesus said, *"I am the God of Abraham."* (Mt. 22:32) He also said, *"Before Abraham was, I Am."* (Jn. 8:58)

As we can see from the scriptures, Abraham was a major focus point, a window of God's heavenly interaction with mankind.

Chapter Two

THE EASTERN GATE   Part 5

WINDOW. No.3   JESUS CHRIST - Northern Window

Window number three represents God's greatest focus point of interaction with planet earth, the manifestation of God's mercy and grace portrayed in Jesus Christ.

The crucifixion and resurrection of Christ are the major focus points of window number three.

The manifestation of the church, and the merging of Jew and Gentile faith are also set in motion in window number three. In the midnight hour of The Night Watch, Jesus Christ the Light of heaven penetrates the darkness of a wicked world. Heaven declares Emmanuel is born *"Peace on Earth Goodwill to Men."*

WINDOW. No.4   THE GLORIOUS CHURCH - Eastern Window

Window number four represents the closing of the church age and the establishment of the Kingdom of God on earth. We are now in the **Twilight Zone** between two ages, awaiting the final fulfillment of God's judgment on the world antichrist system. The **eastern window** corresponds with the Eastern Gate, and represents God's way out for His church, His espoused bride. **The Eastern Gate is biblically consistent with the entrance to God's presence.** Window **number four** is the last window of opportunity to escape the coming wrath of God; **this window represents blessing and cursing, judgment and salvation.** Now is the day of salvation, now is the time to repent from our wicked ways as God gathers His final harvest.

Let me explain the "Twilight Zone"

(Oxford Dictionary) *When the sun is just below the horizon in the morning or evening, a period of faint light, dimly illuminated, a state of imperfect knowledge or understanding.*

The fluctuation or vacillation of the Prophetic Compass needle represents a period I call the Twilight Zone. This is the period preceding each major intervention of God on the earth.

The Twilight Zone is a form of matrix, a place of development for the coming event, **the stage preparation for heavens next performance.**

The Twilight Zone is the period of transition between the four time frames or ages.

For example:

- A family to a nation
- The merging of Jew and Gentile as one in the faith
- The world system transferred to the Kingdom of Christ on earth
- Mortal man puts on immortality

The church is in a place of transition right now, the Twilight Zone between two dispensations.

The stage is being set for the coming event and heavens next performance. The final window of God's power and manifestation is about to open. This generation is about to experience another major window of heavenly interaction with mankind.

We are the Children of the East, Kings and Priests of the Most High God. This is our window of opportunity, *"don't miss this hour of His visitation."*

Chapter Two

THE EASTERN GATE   Part 6

THE TABERNACLE

The Tabernacle entrance was facing EAST. Once again this is significant to The Night Watch as the gateway of salvation and the eternal presence of God. God has provided a place of intimacy beyond the veil of human flesh, a place we can dwell, a place of perfect peace, even in the midst of turmoil and distress.

There is a process of entering this glorious realm of His presence.

➤ **Firstly** in the courtyard we approach the **Sacrificial Altar**, the place of repentance and acceptance. The sacrificial altar represents **SALVATION** by the blood of Christ.

➤ **Secondly** in the courtyard we approach the **Brass Water Basin**, the place of personal reflection and cleansing of the priests. The brass water basin represents the believers **WATER BAPTISM,** the cleansing and regeneration of the soul. **Buried with Him in baptism, raised with Him through the faith of the operation of God.** (Col.2:12)

➤ **Thirdly** we enter **The Sanctuary**, where the ordinances of divine service took place by the priests. (Heb. 9) The sanctuary of divine service represents the **HOLY GHOST ANOINTING** of the believer. The sanctuary is the place of spiritual preparation and renewing of the mind. The place of conditioning the heart for intimate fellowship with God, beyond the veil in the chambers of the Lord.

➤ **Fourthly The Holy of Holies,** the gateway to heaven. The believers right to enter the Holiest place is based on the sacrificial blood of Jesus Christ, the Lamb of God. By His own blood once and for all He has entered the Holy place, having obtained eternal redemption for us. (Heb. 9:12)

I believe the Holy of Holies is the **launching pad** for the body of Christ into eternity. **The departure lounge** for His glorious church, security checks have taken place and Holy Ghost scanning for foreign objects is complete. **Nothing that is defiled shall enter the Kingdom of God.** (Rev. 21:27)

Chapter Two

THE EASTERN GATE   Part 7

THE HOLY OF HOLIES

The Holy of Holies is the place where two worlds meet. We must know Him and experience His presence this side of eternity.

Let me remind you once again that the needle on the Prophetic Compass is pointing **directly east right now**, the dawning of the **seventh millennium.** Departure lights are flashing and final calls are heralding for immediate response, gates will be closed on His arrival and departure will take place in the twinkling of an eye.

THE ISRAELITE CAMP *Interesting note!*

When the Israelites set up camp around the Tabernacle, the total number of men twenty years and over was 603,550 this did not include woman and children. Three tribes on each side according to their numbers actually formed a **cross like formation** visible from higher ground.

God's redemption through the cross is continually visible throughout scripture from beginning to end. Amen!

See Diagram: **THE ISRAELITE CAMP** FORMATION - The form of a cross.

THE ISRAELITE CAMP FORMATION - The Form of a Cross.

As you can see on this diagram, the set up of the Israelite camp formed a cross like formation visible from higher ground. This was a prophetic demonstration unknown to the Hebrew people of the coming of Christ, and the salvation of the cross.

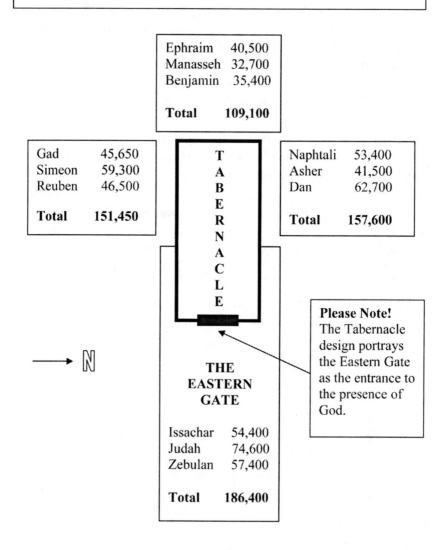

Ephraim	40,500
Manasseh	32,700
Benjamin	35,400
Total	**109,100**

Gad	45,650
Simeon	59,300
Reuben	46,500
Total	**151,450**

TABERNACLE

Naphtali	53,400
Asher	41,500
Dan	62,700
Total	**157,600**

Please Note! The Tabernacle design portrays the Eastern Gate as the entrance to the presence of God.

THE EASTERN GATE

Issachar	54,400
Judah	74,600
Zebulan	57,400
Total	**186,400**

N

Chapter Three

THE HEBREW HARVESTS
Part 1

GOD'S TOTAL HARVEST PLAN

During my times of study I came across a Hebrew harvest calendar. I was amazed at the incredible significance the calendar represented when placed upon the **Prophetic Time Clock.**

The twelve-month Hebrew harvest calendar represented God's total harvest plan for planet earth from beginning to end.

The significance of PLOWING, SOWING, BLOSSOM, AND HARVESTING have an incredible significance when placed upon the **Prophetic Time Clock.**

> ➤ The season of **plowing, sowing, and blossom,** represent God's ground preparation and foundational structure for the church.
> ➤ The **harvesting season** parallels on the **Prophetic Time Clock** with the appearance of Jesus Christ the Messiah.

Harvesting represents the initiation of the church age and the beginning of the temple structure. *"I will build my church and the gates of hell shall not prevail against it!"* (Mt. 16:18)

Harvesting continues to the **olive season** in the millennial reign of Christ, the completion and perfection of His glorious church on earth.

The barley, the wheat, the early figs, the grape, and the olive, all have an individual significance in the time frames of The Night Watch.

See Diagram: **THE HEBREW HARVESTS** - God's total harvest plan.

THE HEBREW HARVESTS - God's Total Harvest Plan.

When the **Hebrew Harvest Season** is placed on the Prophetic Time Clock, **God's total harvest plan is revealed.** Each aspect of the harvest season reveals an incredible significance between natural and spiritual events.

The birth of Jesus Christ parallels with the beginning of the harvest season, **He is the Lord of the Harvest.**

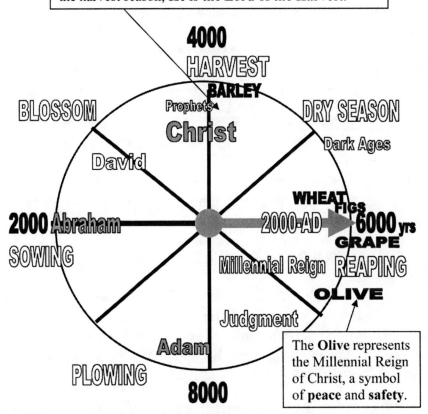

The **Olive** represents the Millennial Reign of Christ, a symbol of **peace** and **safety.**

The gathering of the **Wheat** is the beginning of the end-time harvest. The gathering of the **Figs** represents the re-establishment of Israel. The year 2000-AD is parallel with the final harvest season. God is about to thrust in His sickle and reap His long awaited sweet **Grapes**. The **Grapes** portray the Rapture and Resurrection of the Saints.

Chapter Three

THE HEBREW HARVESTS   Part 2

THE SEASONS AND THEIR TIME FRAMES

Let me explain the significance of the seasons and their time frames, according to The Night Watch revelation.

PLOWING **3000-BC**. Represents the ground preparation and cultivation of a holy seed, set apart for the purposes of God, the formation of a family line through which the Messiah would come. This bloodline and spiritual seed was represented initially in Adam, Seth, Enoch, Noah, and the family of Abraham.

SOWING **2000-BC**. Represents Abraham, the seed of a nation, and the father of our faith. Abraham believed God and it was counted unto him for righteousness. Abraham represents New Testament salvation found only by faith in the Lord Jesus Christ. Abraham, Isaac, and Jacob represent the birthing of a future nation through the covenant promises of God.

BLOSSOM **1000-BC**. (The almond blossom is a symbol of hope and new life.)

In parallel to The Night Watch, Israel was in blossom at this time as a united nation with great power and blessing under the reign of King David and King Solomon. The almond blossom also represented the future hope and new life found only in Jesus Christ, the Lord of the coming harvest.

THE BARLEY HARVEST - **FIRST CENTURY AD. How significant that the harvest season begins with the appearance of Jesus Christ on the Hebrew harvest calendar.**

The barley harvest, the first of the grains, the poor mans bread. Jesus is represented here as the bread to the poor in the feeding of the five thousand with the five barley loaves and two small fishes.

(Jn. 6:9) Jesus was born in Bethlehem, which also means *House of Bread*.

THE DRY SEASON **500-1500-AD**

In parallel to The Night Watch, the dry season represents the Middle Ages, medieval times, and the dark ages of religious persecution. The dry season also represents decline, and the falling away of the Christian faith, due to persecution and lack of biblical truths.

THE WHEAT HARVEST **1800-1900-AD** (The Feast of Weeks) PENTECOST

The wheat harvest represents **the beginning of the final world harvest**. Biblical truths are restored, and the Christian church begins reformation. The Feast of Weeks or Pentecost represents the dedication of the harvest to God, the provider of all blessings. The **Feast of Pentecost** also parallels with the PENTECOSTAL MOVEMENT in the early 1900s-AD.

Chapter Three

THE HEBREW HARVESTS   Part 3

THE FIG TREE (A Symbol of peace and blessing)
The fig tree many times was used as a symbol of Israel. (Jer. 24:1-8 Hos. 9:10)
The green fig appeared in April around the time of the Passover. This was significant of Israel's rejection of Christ. *Note* the cursing of the fig tree by Jesus in (Mat. 21:18-21) and also the judgment on the non-fruit bearing fig tree. (Lk.13: 6-9)

THE EARLY FIGS OR FIRST RIPE FIGS – 1900-AD
The Night Watch parallel of the early figs in June represents the reinstatement of the nation of Israel in May 1948 and the return of the Jewish people to their home land.

Israel must be re-established to fulfill God's word concerning:
> The return and salvation of the Jews:
> The rebuilding of the temple site and re-establishment of the Jewish traditions:
> The abomination of the antichrist and the judgment of all nations:

THE GRAPE HARVEST (The grape is also a symbol of peace and blessing)
Every man dwelt safely under his vine and fig tree. (1 Kings 4:25)
The grapevine is the most common, best known and best loved of all plants in the Bible. Grape vines were cultivated personally by their owners or by hired hands. God is also our personal husbandman and vinedresser. *"I am the vine, you are the branches"* (Jn.15: 5)
Scripture references concerning the grapevine extend from the days of Noah to the days before the return of Christ. (Gen. 9:20-21) - (Rev. 14:18)

THE SWEET GRAPES

The grapevine represents the Old and New Testament church, God's preparation and tending of the vine for the final reaping of His beloved vineyard.

The instant reaping of the earth in (Rev. 14:14-16) in my opinion is the <u>catching up or rapture</u> of the church, the long awaited **sweet grapes** of the vineyard of the Lord.

*Thou has brought a vine out of Egypt: thou has cast out the heathen, and planted it. Thou prepared room before it, and caused it to take deep root, **and it filled the land.*** (Ps. 80:8,9)

THE WILD GRAPES

The wild grapes represent rebellion, unbelief and the rejection of God's grace and salvation.

Judgment of the wild grapes cast into the wine press of God's anger is the judgment of the nations. This will take place at the end of the tribulation period at the battle of Armageddon. (Rev. 14:17-20) God was disappointed with Israel for producing **wild grapes;** wild grapes are a symbol of disobedience and rebellion. (Is. 5:1-7)

Chapter Three

THE HEBREW HARVESTS   Part 4

THE OLIVE HARVEST (The olive is the emblem of peace, safety, blessing and prosperity.)

The olive is one of the most beautiful and valuable of all Bible trees.

The cultivation of the olive tree required much time, toil, and patience. The olive tree bares no fruit for 3-4 years, and no plentiful harvest for 16-18 years, during which time the tree requires careful attention. A properly cared for, full sized tree will produce half a ton of oil per year, and continue until it reaches an incredible age. The destruction or failure of the olive tree was regarded as the utmost disaster.

THE SPIRITUAL SIGNIFICANCE OF THE OLIVE

- ➤ The olive is a symbol of new life, the olive leaf marked the end of the flood and the beginning of a new age (Gen. 8:11)
- ➤ The olive is likened unto the Promised Land (Deut. 6:11 8:8)
- ➤ The anointing oil of kings and priests (1Sam. 10:1) (Ps. 45:7) (Lev. 8:10,30)
- ➤ The anointing oil of the New Testament church (Jam. 5:14)
- ➤ Christ ascended from the Mount of Olives, and also suffered in the Garden of Gethsemane. Meaning *(The Olive Press)*
- ➤ The seven candlestick Menorah was fueled by olive oil in the Tabernacle.
- ➤ The olive portrays Christ as the Anointed One.
- ➤ The two witnesses in the book of Revelations are portrayed as two olive trees. (Rev. 11:4)

THE OLIVE - A SYMBOL OF THE MILLENNIAL REIGN OF CHRIST

The significance of the olive harvest and The Night Watch revelation is the parallel of the seventh day. **The season of the olive harvest is parallel with the millennial reign of Christ on the Prophetic Time Clock.** The olive is the emblem of peace, safety, and prosperity; the emblems of peace and safety can only be fulfilled during the millennial reign of Jesus Christ. He is the Prince of Peace. *"That's exciting news!"*

Chapter Three

THE HEBREW HARVESTS   Part 5

THE PROPHETIC CALENDAR

This is a diagram incorporating the Hebrew and equivalent modern day calendar.

The month of *Nisan* is the first month of the Hebrew calendar.

The seventh month of *Tishri* was classed as the first month of the financial year, or **the beginning of a new season. This parallels with the beginning of creation, and the conception of mankind on the Prophetic Time Clock.** *See diagram:* The Hebrew Harvests

The 20th century church is situated on the Harvest Calendar between the Hebrew months of *Sivan* and *Tammuz* or June on the modern day calendar. This period also parallels on the **Prophetic Time Clock** with **6000 years** of biblical history.

The numbers **1-12** represent a twelve-month harvest season, beginning at the month of *Tishri*. The 20th century church also parallels with the ninth month of the harvest season.

The ninth month also represents the human birth cycle, in other words the church is in her fullness of time, and the Kingdom of God is about to be delivered.

See Diagram: **THE PROPHETIC CALENDAR -** Hebrew and modern.

THE PROPHETIC CALENDAR - Hebrew and Modern Day.

The Church Age in the 20th Century AD is parallel with the <u>ninth month</u> of the Hebrew Harvest Season and the <u>ninth hour</u> of the Night Watch. Number nine represents the human birth cycle. The Church is pregnant with the Kingdom of God and about to be delivered of her child. **Note!** Number <u>nine</u> also denotes divine judgment, judgment is coming on the World Antichrist System.

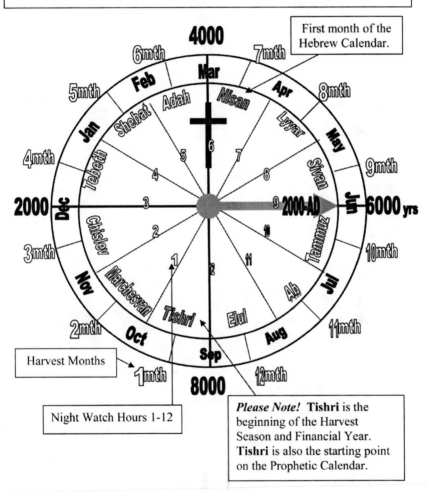

First month of the Hebrew Calendar.

Harvest Months

Night Watch Hours 1-12

Please Note! **Tishri** is the beginning of the Harvest Season and Financial Year. **Tishri** is also the starting point on the Prophetic Calendar.

Chapter Four

THE HEBREW FEASTS
Part 1

FEAST REPRESENTATIONS

THE PASSOVER FEAST

God commanded the children of Israel to sacrifice a lamb and put the blood on the doorposts of their houses. This would protect each family from the angel of death, and the judgment of God on the land of Egypt. They were then told to roast and eat the lamb in celebration of their freedom. **From the Christian prospective Jesus Christ represents God's sacrificial Lamb for the whole world. The crucifixion of Christ actually took place as the Jews prepared for the Passover Feast. The very Lamb of God was fulfilling scriptural prophecy in their midst.** Jesus being dead was removed from the cross due to the preparation of the Passover Feast on the following day.

THE FEAST OF UNLEAVENED BREAD

To the Jews this was the remembrance of the bread of affliction and the bondage of Egypt. For the Christian this represents Christ the Sinless One. Leaven is descriptive of sin in our lives. (1Cor. 5:7,8). Christ being sinless is represented by the **unleavened bread.**

It also represents the bread of affliction and the bitterness of His cross.

THE FEAST OF FIRSTFRUITS

The firstfruits of the harvest are given to God. (Lev. 23:10) The Feast of Firstfruits took place on the first day after the Passover Sabbath. **Incredibly this was the day that Jesus rose from the dead.** (Mk. 16:1-6) Jesus is the firstfruits of the glorious resurrection. (1Cor. 15:20-23) This mortal must put on immortality. (1Cor. 15:53,54)

THE WHEAT HARVEST (The Feast of Weeks or Pentecost)

This is a one-day feast celebrating the wheat harvest. Two loaves were traditionally waived before the Lord, and offered for the people as a dedication of the wheat harvest. Two loaves from a Christian prospective could represent Jew and Gentile believers made one in Christ.

Pentecost, *Greek for fiftieth* derived its name from the fact that it was celebrated seven weeks or fifty days after the Passover.

The Wheat harvest represents the beginning of the end time harvest. The wheat begins the final gathering of things in heaven and things on earth, the severing of the chaff, the purging of wickedness from the house of God, and the preparation of a glorious church.

The position on the **Prophetic Time Clock** for this feast is the late 1800s AD and represents the dawning of revival and charismatic renewal in the church.

The early church was birthed on the day of Pentecost in Acts chapter two. I believe the greatest manifestation of God is yet to come upon this generation. Christ in us, the hope of glory is about to be revealed in power through His glorious church.

Chapter Four

THE HEBREW FEASTS   Part 2

NEW BEGINNINGS

According to the **Prophetic Time Clock** the following feasts parallel with the seventh month of *Tishri* on the Hebrew calendar. **The seventh month is classed as the beginning of the Jewish financial year; this would indicate a time of new beginnings prophetically.**

The following feasts are positioned at the end of the forth watch or the beginning of the ninth day which signifies the end of the old and the beginning of the new.

➢ **The Day of Atonement:** Judgment is now complete!

➢ **The Feast of Tabernacles:** God forever will dwell in the midst of His people.

➢ **The Feast of Trumpets:** The ram's horn declaring a new heaven and a new earth.

These feasts represent a new beginning for the Eternal Kingdom of God. Christ has ruled in victory, judged in righteousness, and behold He makes all things new.

Nevertheless we, according to His promise, look for new heavens and a new earth, wherein dwells righteousness. (2Pet. 3:11-13)

The position of the Hebrew Feasts on the **Prophetic Time Clock**, represent three major celebrations for the Christian church.

➢ The birth of Christ

➢ The final harvest and resurrection of the church

➢ The establishment of the eternal Kingdom of God

See Diagram: **THE HEBREW FEASTS** - Three major celebrations.

THE HEBREW FEASTS - Three Major Celebrations.

The position of the Hebrew Feasts on the Prophetic Time Clock represents Three Major Celebrations for the Christian Church.
No. 1 Salvation of God in Christ
No. 2 Final Harvest of the Church Age and The Resurrection
No. 3 Establishment of the Eternal Kingdom of God on Earth

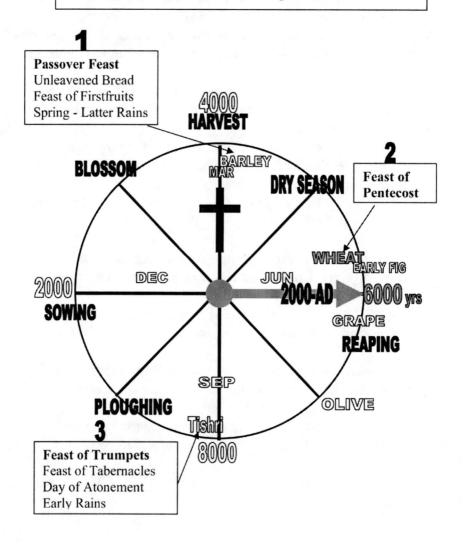

1

Passover Feast
Unleavened Bread
Feast of Firstfruits
Spring - Latter Rains

2

Feast of Pentecost

3

Feast of Trumpets
Feast of Tabernacles
Day of Atonement
Early Rains

Chapter Five

THE MENORAH
Part 1

SEVEN GOLDEN CANDLESTICKS

The seven golden candlesticks situated in the Holy Place of the Tabernacle, represent the seven days of creation, and the perfection of God the eternal light. The Menorah was beaten from one piece of solid gold and it burned with oil continually. The New Testament portrays Jesus Christ as the source of light itself. (Jn. 1:1-5)

Jesus said *"I am the light of the world: he that follows me shall not walk in darkness, but shall have the light of life."* (Jn. 8:12) In the book of Revelation Jesus is seen standing in the midst of the seven candlesticks that represent the seven churches. (Rev. 1:12-20)

In respect to The Night Watch and the significance of the Menorah, **Jesus is represented as the fourth or center stem of the candlestick, the light to the world for both the Old and New Testament**. His life is the light of men from beginning to end. *In him was life; and the life was the light of men.* (Jn. 1:4)

SEVEN DISPENSATIONS OR CHURCH AGES

Jesus standing in the midst of the seven candlesticks or churches can also represent **seven dispensations**, or **seven church ages** from Adam to the millennial reign of Christ. On the **Prophetic Time**

Clock the seven golden candlesticks are figurative of **7000 years** of extended light and salvation. The millennial reign of Christ represents the perfection and completion of His glorious church on earth. (Seven is the number of completion and perfection.)

See Diagram: **SEVEN CANDLESTICK MENORAH -** The perfection of a glorious church.

SEVEN CANDLSTICK MENORAH - The Perfection of the Church.

The **Seven Candlestick Menorah** represents a period of
7000 years. Seven church ages or dispensations designated for
the completion and perfection of a Glorious Church on earth.
Seven denotes the number of completion and perfection.

Jesus Christ is represented as the
Center Candlestick. Rev.1:13
He is the Light of the world for the
Old and New Testament Saints.

THE MENORAH

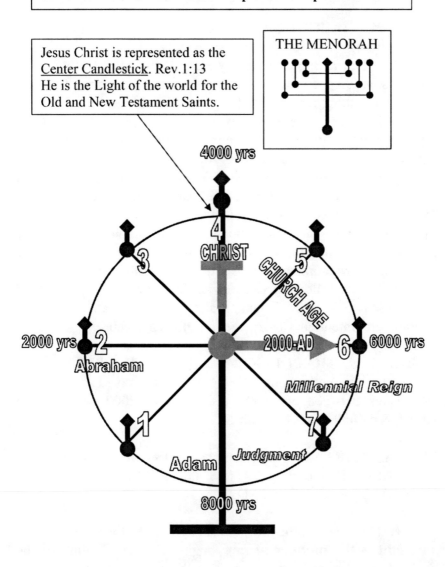

Chapter Five

THE MENORAH   Part 2

NINE CANDLESTICK HANUKKAH - (Menorah)

HANUKKAH –EIGHT DAY FESTIVAL

According to tradition, approximately 165 BC Matttityahu (Matthew) Patriarch of the priestly Hasamonian clan, supported by his five sons, stepped forward to challenge the Greek army.

In the continuing process his son Judah Maccabees liberated Jerusalem and reclaimed the Holy temple. He cleared the temple of idols, rebuilt the altar, and prepared to resume divine service. Jewish legend states at the rededication of the temple, only one small cruse of sacred olive oil could be found, **only one day's supply of oil for the eight days of dedication**. Regardless of the circumstance Maccabees proceeded to dedicate the temple. He lit the lamps of the Menorah with the small amount of oil available. Miraculously as if to confirm their faith and victory, the oil did not burn out. The flames of the Menorah shone brightly for the full eight days of the dedication. The following year Jewish Sages officially proclaimed the eight-day festival of Hanukkah, as a yearly celebration. This was to commemorate their victory over religious persecution.

TOTAL DURATION OF GOD'S REDEMPTIVE PLAN

On the **Prophetic Time Clock** Christ is portrayed as the center candlestick between two **4000 year** periods, **4000 years** before Christ, and **4000 years** after Christ.

THE APPEARANCE OF CHRIST ON PLANET EARTH LITERALLY DIVIDED EARTH'S TIME FRAME INTO TWO SEPERATE ERAS, BC and AD.

Four (4) is the number of the earth, two times four is eight.

Eight is the number of new beginnings, and completes the cycle of events contained in The Night Watch revelation.

Christ is the support stem and center candlestick of the Menorah. The other candles are lit from the center candle. Jesus is portrayed here as the light bearer of past and future generations. **This is clearly demonstrated by four candles each side of Christ in the nine candlestick Hanukkah** – Menorah.

See Diagram: **NINE CANDLESTICK HANUKKAH -** God's total redemption plan.

NINE CANDLESTICK HANUKKAH - God's Total Redemption Plan.

The Nine Candlestick Hanukkah, represents God's total plan of Salvation. **8000 years** of extended light for the redemption of all mankind. **Eight is the number of new beginnings and purification. Nine denotes the divine judgment of God is complete.**

Note!
Christ is portrayed as the <u>Center Candlestick</u> between two 4000-year periods, BC-AD

THE HANUKKAH

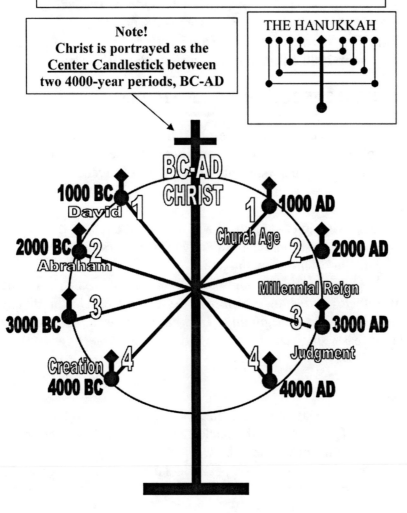

Chapter Five

THE MENORAH   Part 3

NINE MONTHS OF PREGNANCY
Nine Candlesticks also represent nine months of pregnancy, from creation to the birth of the New Kingdom. According to the Prophetic Time Clock we are at the ninth month of the harvest season. Nine months is also parallel with 6000 years of biblical history, year 2000 AD. *See Diagram:* The Prophetic Calendar

NINE DENOTES JUDGMENT AND DEVINE COMPLETENESS
We are in the season of the ninth harvest month according to the Prophetic Calendar. This is significant to the Judgment of the nations arrayed against Israel at the battle of Armageddon.

Note!

Final and complete judgment will be carried out after the millennial reign of Christ, on the eighth day **(8000 years)** from Adam, at the Great White Throne of Judgment.

At the beginning of the ninth day **(9000 years)** on the **Prophetic Time Clock**, divine judgment will be complete. The ninth day corresponds with the beginning of the harvest season, and the three Hebrew feasts that represent a new beginning. *See Diagram*: The Hebrew Feasts

Example:

> ➤ The Day of Atonement: Judgment is now complete!
> ➤ The Feast of Tabernacles: God forever will dwell in the midst of His people.
> ➤ The Feast of Trumpets: Declaring a new heaven and a new earth.

Chapter Five

THE MENORAH   Part 4

BOTH CANDLESTICKS REPRESENT A DURATION OF TIME

SEVEN CANDLESTICKS

The seven candlesticks represent a period of **7000 years,** from Adam to the end of the millennial reign of Christ. This completes the establishment and perfection of a glorious church on earth. After God's judgment on the world antichrist system, Christ and His saints will rule for **1000 years** over those who remain.

NINE CANDLESTICKS

The four candlesticks on each side of the Hanukkah represent **8000 years** of extended grace, the total plan of God's redemption on the **Prophetic Time Clock.** Christ is portrayed as the center stem of the Hanukkah. He is the light bearer that stands in the midst of two **4000 year** periods, **4000-BC** and **4000-AD.** Four is the number of the earth, before and after Christ.

Each candlestick represents a time frame of God's extended light and grace.

Nine candlesticks also declare that complete and final judgment has taken place at the Great White Throne of Judgment. Judgment takes place after the millennial reign of Christ on the eighth day of the **Prophetic Time Clock.** (Number nine, denotes: Finality of Judgment 3x3, the product of divine completeness.)

EIGHT DAYS OF EXTENDED GRACE

As previously discussed, Judah Maccabees was in the process of rededicating the temple in 165 BC. The Hanukkah - Menorah burned continually for the full eight days of dedication with only enough oil for one day. *Let me share an interesting thought!*

Because of sin, mans existence was not to extend beyond **1000 years,** mans eternal destiny was reduced to one day, *one day with the*

Lord is as a thousand years. (2Pet. 3:8) God said to Adam, *"in the day that you eat of this fruit **you** shall die."* (Gen. 2:17) Adam died at the age of nine hundred and thirty years and did not complete a day, **(1000 years.)** No man thereafter lived to be a thousand years.

The candlestick of man that should have only lasted a day was prolonged for eight days.

I believe this is significant to 8000 years of extended grace for planet earth.

The candle of mankind was snuffed out by sin and reduced to only one day's oil, but **by the grace God** the light of humanity will burn continuously for the full eight days **(8000 years.)**

This completes the cycle of the Night Watch, and fulfills God's total plan of redemption for all mankind.

Eight is the number of new beginnings or commencement.

And I saw a new heaven and a new earth: for the first heaven and the first earth were passed away and there was no more sea. (Rev. 21:1)

*And He that sat upon the throne said, **"Behold, I make all things new."*** (Rev. 21:5)

Chapter Five

THE MENORAH   Part 5

EIGHT DAYS OF PURIFICATION
Eight is the number of cleansing and purification.

CLEANSING OF THE TEMPLE
Eight days was allotted for the cleansing of the temple.
So they sanctified the house of the Lord in EIGHT DAYS.
(2Chron. 29: 16-18)

We as the temple of God are undergoing the process of purification by the Holy Spirit.
We are being prepared for our appointment with the King of Kings and Lord of Lords.

CLEANSING OF CIRCUMCISION
Circumcision is a form of cleansing, the cutting away of the flesh, the covenant of separation from a world of sin. Abraham was given the covenant of circumcision and **circumcised Isaac on the eighth day** (Acts 7:8) Circumcision is an everlasting covenant. (Gen. 17:12,13)
Jesus was circumcised on the eighth day. (Lk. 2:21) As Christians we undergo the circumcision of the heart by faith in Jesus Christ. (Rom. 2:29)

CLEANSING OF BAPTISM
Jesus was water baptized to fulfill all righteousness. (Mt. 3:13) Jesus being sinless calls us to follow Him through the process of water baptism and the purification of the heart by the infilling of the Holy Spirit. We are washed in the Blood of the Lamb.

THE FURNACE - God's kiln of purification
I believe that eight days has been allotted to purify the earth in God's kiln of purification.

His vessels of honor shall be removed from the kiln of purification at the appointed time.

Only those who hear the voice of the Son of God shall be taken out of the kiln at the resurrection of life. Those who **hear not** the voice of the Son of God shall remain in the kiln, awaiting final damnation.

FIRST-THE CLEANSING OF WATER

*And God spared not the old world, but saved Noah **the eighth person**, a preacher of righteousness, bringing in the flood upon the world of the ungodly.* (2Pet. 2:5) Eight souls were **saved by water.** (1Pet. 3:20)

THE SAME WATER THAT CARRIED THE RIGHTEOUS TO SAFETY ALSO DESTROYED THE WICKED.

SECOND -THE PURIFICATION OF FIRE

The final purification of the earth will be by fire.

But the day of the Lord will come as a thief in the night; in the which the heavens shall pass away with a great noise, and the elements shall melt with fervent heat, the earth also and the works that are therein shall be burned up. Seeing then that all these things shall be dissolved, what manner of persons ought ye to be in all holy conversation and godliness. Looking for and hasting unto the coming of the day of God, wherein the heavens being on fire shall be dissolved, and the elements shall melt with fervent heat? Nevertheless we, according to his promise, look for new heavens and a new earth, wherein dwells righteousness. (2Pet. 3:10-13)

THE SAME FIRE THAT PURIFIES THE RIGHTEOUS, WILL ALSO CONSUME THE UNGODLY.

Chapter Five

THE MENORAH   Part 6

CHRIST THE LIGHT BEARER

JESUS CHRIST is the center stem of each candlestick, HE IS THE LIGHT BEARER.

There is no escaping the darkness without the Light Bearer. Only He can lead you through the valley of the shadow of death. He is the Light of Life, the Door, the Exodus, the only escape hatch on a vessel doomed for the depths of hell and a lost eternity.

He is a lamp unto your feet and without His light there is no escaping the gross darkness that overshadows the world. He is **the only way out.** He is the Light Bearer.

THE CANDLESTICKS ARE EXTENSIONS OF GOD'S LIGHT, PIERCING THE ETERNAL DARKNESS WITH A PERIOD OF MERCY AND GRACE.

CHRIST THE BRANCH

Behold, I will bring forth my servant THE BRANCH. (Zec.3:8)

*And there shall come forth a rod out of the stem of Jesse and **a Branch** shall grow out of his roots: **And the spirit of the Lord shall rest upon him, the spirit of wisdom and understanding, the spirit of counsel and might, the spirit of knowledge and of the fear of the Lord.** (Is.11: 1, 2)*

THE TABERNACLE MENORAH

The Tabernacle menorah was shaped in the form of an almond tree. The almond tree portrays Christ as a symbol of hope and new life. There is only one tree of life.

We were once cut off and alienated from the life of God, disconnected from the branch, dying and withering away. Only the blood washed believer can be grafted into the **eternal stem of salvation** and live again.

The original tree of life was not accessible due to the corruption of man. God in His mercy through the blood of Christ has extended His love and given the world a grace period of **8000 years** to once again partake of the tree of life, which is Christ Himself.

The eight branches of the Hanukkah represent the arms of God's salvation, extended out with light and life for all mankind.

Chapter Six

THE CROSS
Part 1

SIX HOURS ON THE CROSS
And it was THE THIRD HOUR, and they crucified Him. (Mk.15: 25)

Jesus was on the cross from the **third hour** till the **ninth hour** or 9am till 3pm.

As you can see from the diagram of The Cross, this covers a six-hour period. Six is the number of man, the exact period from Abraham 2000-BC to the closing of the church age 2000-AD. I say the closing of the Church Age, because Jesus said that those who witness the re-establishment of the nation of Israel would see the fulfillment of the **gentile church age.** (Lk. 21:24) This is an exciting time to be alive! The blood of the Lamb is effective on both sides of the cross, those who lived in the shadow and hope of it, and those who live in the light and reality of it. **His blood covers both the Old and New Testament Saints.** *"Hallelujah!"*

DARKNESS AT MIDDAY (Supernatural Phenomena)
Now from THE SIXTH HOUR there was DARKNESS over all the land unto THE NINTH HOUR. (Mt. 27:45)

Once again looking at the diagram of The Cross, I believe God was supernaturally demonstrating a time period for the church age.

I believe God was saying that darkness or the reign of Satan would continue for the next **2000 years,** the closing of the 3rd Watch on the **Prophetic Time Clock**. This would complete the period of the church age and lead us into the seventh millennium corresponding with the fourth or morning watch on the **Prophetic Time Clock**. The morning watch is the breaking forth of a new day, the day of the Lord. This is the darkest hour for an unbelieving world, and the most glorious hour for the church of the Living God. I can see it now, the flickering glow of His glory on the horizon, rise and shine for your light is come and the glory of the Lord is risen upon you.

It was the midnight hour when Jesus Christ appeared on the **Prophetic Time Clock**. Paul could see the night was far spent and the morning watch was soon approaching.

I believe the morning watch is dedicated to Jesus Christ and His glorious church.

Chapter Six

THE CROSS   **Part 2**

THE NINTH HOUR

And about THE NINTH HOUR Jesus cried with a loud voice, saying, "Eli, Eli, lama sabachthani?" that is to say, My God, my God, why hast thou forsaken me?

Jesus, when He had cried again with a loud voice, yielded up the ghost (died) (Mt. 27:46-50)

At the NINTH HOUR Jesus cried, *"it is finished!"* (Jn. 19:30) I believe Jesus was looking from the cross to the end of the church age and with His last breath proclaims prophetic judgment on the antichrist system, *"IT IS FINISHED!"* devil your lease is up on planet earth, and I hereby give you notice.

And, behold, the veil of the temple was rent in twain from the top to the bottom; and the earth did quake, and the rocks rent; (Mt. 27:51) This verse indicates that access into the holy place or presence of God is now made available through the shed blood of Jesus Christ, the Lamb of God. Heaven has opened its doors for all who would believe.

And the graves were opened; and many bodies of the saints which slept arose, and came out of the graves after his resurrection, and went into the holy city, and appeared unto many. (Mt. 27:52-53) This scripture is a prophetic reference to the soon coming resurrection of the saints.

Darkness will prevail to the ninth hour **2000-AD** then resurrection light will break forth.

"Get ready saints!" The ninth hour prophetically is upon this generation.

The ninth hour is the Jewish hour of prayer, how fitting at this time for God to re-establish prayer as the basis for His glorious Church. *My house shall be called a house of prayer.* (Mt. 21:13)

The ninth hour is very significant to The Night Watch prophetically!

➤ The ninth hour is the year **2000-AD** on the Prophetic Time Clock.

➤ The ninth hour parallels with the ninth month on the Hebrew harvest calendar.

➤ The ninth hour is **the end of day six** on the **Prophetic time Clock**.

➤ (Six is the number of man and God finished His work on the sixth day.)

➤ The ninth hour represents the birth cycle, and the Kingdom of God is about to be birthed.

➤ The ninth hour parallels with **the Jewish hour of prayer,** 3pm our time.

➤ God is re-establishing His house as a house of prayer, not merchandise.

➤ God's greatest manifestation will be birthed by a praying generation.

THE NINTH HOUR HAS COME
THE DAWNING OF THE SEVENTH DAY
THE MORNING OF THE RESURRECTION THIRD DAY
THE HOUR OF PRAYER
IT'S THE MORNING WATCH AND THE COCK IS ABOUT
TO CROW
THE ALARM CLOCK OF HEAVEN IS ABOUT TO SOUND
"WAKE UP CHURCH!"

THE CROSS - Six Hours on the Cross - The Number of Man.

> **Jesus was six hours on the cross,** from 9am till 3pm. From Abraham 2000-BC to the closing of the Church Age 2000-AD. This six-hour period represents the salvation of the Old and New Testament Saints.

> **Supernatural Darkness from midday till 3pm.** I believe this was a prophetic indication that Satan's rule of darkness would continue till 3pm or 2000-AD. This would complete a period of 6000 years of satanic dominion.

6th Hour
midday
CHRIST Church Age
DARKNESS

3rd hr
9 am
2000-BC
Abraham

2000-AD
9th hr
3 pm
Millennial Reign

Judgment

1st hr
6 am

12th hr
6 pm

Chapter Seven

SIGNIFICANCE OF THE TEMPLE
Part 1

GOD'S TRUE DWELLING PLACE

God's true dwelling place is in the hearts of men and woman.
Know ye not that ye are the temple of God, and that the Spirit
of God dwells in you? If any man defile the temple of God, him shall
God destroy; *for the temple of God is holy, which temple ye are.*
(1Cor. 3:16,17) *What? know ye not that your body is the temple of
the Holy Ghost which is in you, which ye have of God and ye are not
your own.* (1Cor. 6:19)

A SPIRITUAL TEMPLE

From the seed of Abraham's faith accounted to him as righteousness, the foundation for a spiritual temple was set in motion. Israel
beheld the glory of Solomon's temple, and that was only a shadow
of the coming Kingdom of Christ.

A TEMPLE STRUCTURE IS NOW VISIBLE TO THE 20ᵀᴴ CENTURY CHURCH IN THE FORM OF MOUNT ZION.

- ➤ From the seed of Abraham: **2000-BC**
- ➤ To the birth of Christ: **4000**
- ➤ To the closing of the church age: **2000-AD**

THE TEMPLE - A Complete Structure is Visible of Mt Zion.

Christ is about to return for His Glorious Church,
His Church is represented as the Temple of Zion.
Christ and His redeemed saints will rule and reign
on earth for **1000 years** in the sight of mortal man.

A **complete structure** of
Mt Zion is now visible to
the 20th Century Church.

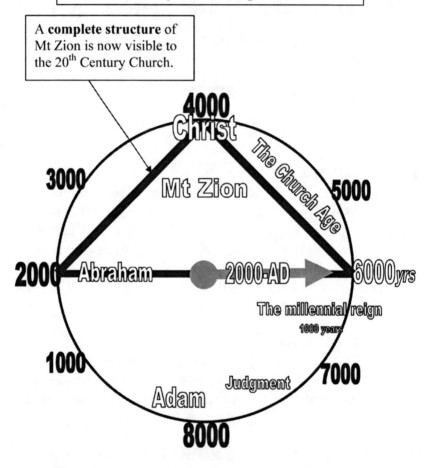

Chapter Seven

THE TEMPLE   Part 2

THE TEMPLE OF ZION - The Church of the Living God

The following verses are an indication of God's great desire to dwell among His people.

Note the spiritual connection between the heavenly and earthly Jerusalem.

For the Lord hath chosen Zion; he hath desired it for his habitation. This is my rest forever: here will I dwell; for I have desired it. I will abundantly bless her provision: I will satisfy her poor with bread. I will also clothe her priests with salvation: and her saints shall shout aloud for joy. (Ps. 132:13-16)

But ye are come unto mount Zion, and unto the city of the living God, the heavenly Jerusalem, and to an innumerable company of angels,

To the general assembly and church of the firstborn, which are written in heaven, and to God the Judge of all, and to the spirits of just men made perfect, (Heb. 12:22)

You are built upon the foundation of the apostles and prophets, Jesus Christ himself being the chief corner stone; In whom all the building fitly framed together grows unto an holy temple in the Lord: In whom you also are built together for an habitation of God through the Spirit. (Eph. 2:20-22)

After this I will return, and will build again the tabernacle of David, which is fallen down; and I will build again the ruins thereof, and I will set it up: That the residue of men might seek after the Lord, and all the Gentiles, upon whom my name is called, saith the Lord, who does all these things. (Acts 15:16-17) (Amos. 9:11)

"Thou that destroyest the temple, and buildest it in three days, save thyself. If thou be the Son of God, come down from the cross." (Mt. 27:40) Three days from the cross prophetically would incorporate the seventh day from Adam on the **Prophetic Time Clock**. The seventh day incorporates the millennial reign of Christ for the completion of the temple, the perfection of His glorious church.

And, behold, the veil of the temple was rent in twain from the top to the bottom and the earth did quake, and the rocks rent; (Mt. 27:51) The renting of the veil in the temple was an indication that the Holy place was now open to all who believe.

Chapter Seven

THE TEMPLE   Part 3

SOLOMON'S TEMPLE

The construction of Solomon's temple took **seven years** to complete, **four years** on the foundation, and **three years** on the temple.

The building of Solomon's temple can also be related to the building of the Christian church.

The foundation of Solomon's temple took **four years**, while the foundation of the church took **4000 years** from Adam to Christ.

The construction of Solomon's temple took **three years** and for the completion of the church it will be **3000 years**

According to our theologians we have fulfilled **6000 years** of biblical history, and now we stand at the dawning of the seventh day.

As Solomon's temple took seven years to complete, I believe the church is entering her seventh day of completion and perfection. As God rested on the seventh day, so shall the church find her rest in the millennial reign of Jesus Christ.

Chapter Eight

THE NINTH MONTH
Part 1

THE BIRTH CANAL

According to the **Prophetic Time Clock** we have entered the ninth month. The ninth month represents the birth cycle of humanity. The bride of Christ is pregnant with the Kingdom of God. From the conception of man to this present day, she has come to the fullness of time.

Her child (the Kingdom of God) waits, as it were in the womb of the world, for her deliverer. The Christian church is now experiencing birth pangs; the children of promise are now assembling at the birth canal, awaiting delivery.

The Old Testament account of Moses and the Red Sea, was a form of **birth canal** for the children of Israel. They left the land of Egypt that resembled their sin, and journeyed to the Promised Land. Pharaoh (a form of Satan), pursued them to the Red Sea, (a form of birth canal) endeavoring to prevent their release and the birth of the nation.

This is figurative of the Christian church assembled at the birth canal, about to be delivered.

Satan will also pursue the Christian church and endeavor to prevent its release to the Kingdom of God. We must not be enticed to linger in the womb of darkness; we must assemble at the birth canal awaiting delivery.

As the waters of the Red Sea broke forth and became the opening, or the gateway to the Promised Land, so shall the waters break forth in the womb of the world, and release the Kingdom of God within us.

THE BIRTH OF A NATION

Before she travailed, she brought forth; before her pain came, she was delivered of a man child.

Who hath heard such a thing? who hath seen such things? **"Shall the earth be made to bring forth in one day? or shall a nation be born at once?"** *for as soon as Zion travailed, she brought forth her children.* **"Shall I bring to the birth and not cause to bring forth? saith the Lord: shall I cause to bring forth and shut the womb?"** **saith thy God.** (Is. 66:7-9)

A PERFECT MAN CHILD (Eph. 4:13)

A nation of believers shall be born at once, revealed as it were in one day. God has brought us to the ninth month of pregnancy, the final stages are being completed for the delivery of a **perfect man child,** the complete and matured body of Christ Himself.

God has brought us thus far by His grace, He has waited long for the precious fruit of the earth. The womb of His creation shall not be shut, but shall bring forth a man child, a nation determined to rule and reign in one Christ Jesus.

Rejoice with Jerusalem and be glad with her, all you that love her: Be delighted with the abundance of her glory. I will extend peace to her like a river and the glory of the Gentiles like a flowing stream. For behold, the Lord will come with fire and with His chariots like a whirlwind, to render His anger with fury and His rebuke with flames of fire. For by fire and by His sword will the Lord plead with all flesh and the slain of the Lord shall be many.

These remaining verses from Isaiah 66 confirm the battle of Armageddon, the judgment of the nations, and the birthing of the Kingdom of God.

Chapter Eight

THE NINTH MONTH   Part 2

THE CHURCH IN TRAVAIL

As you can see in Isaiah chapter 66, Zion is now in travail, due to the fullness of her time. The church of the living God, the bride of Christ is now experiencing **the beginnings of birth pangs.**

Christ is about to sweep His beloved bride off her feet to the marriage supper of the Lamb. Judgment will begin for an unbelieving and wicked world as Christ prepares His beloved bride for the millennial reign and His glorious return to earth.

THE HIDDEN ONES

We are the hidden ones, we are dead, and our life is hid with Christ in God. When Christ who is our life, shall appear, we also shall appear with Him in glory. (Col. 3:3,4) We are God's best kept secret, ready to be revealed in the last time. (1Pet. 1:5) We are the stone cut without hands that destroyed the image of world empires, and became a great mountain, and filled the whole earth. (Dan. 2: 34,35)

THE WOMB OF CREATION

The world in its circular fashion surrounded by water and governed by the existence of time is likened to the womb of God's creation.

MANKIND AND THE CHURCH ARE REPRESENTED AS THE WOMAN

Mankind represented as the **woman** was dedicated and espoused to the Son of God.

God impregnated the **woman** with the ability to reproduce in her own image and likeness. The world representing the womb of creation sits poised between two eternities, past and future. On the sixth day of creation the **woman** was formed by God from the dust of the ground and displayed as a magnificent sculpture void of life.

Now the final touch of the Masters hand, the kiss of life. Heaven stands in awe as God Himself breathes into her nostrils His very own life. She awakes and stands before Him, the ultimate glory of His creation. The **woman** is impregnated with the eternal seed, and the ability to reproduce after her kind.

Chapter Nine

SATAN'S ABORTION PLAN
Part 1

SPIRITUAL ADULTERY

Satan attempted to totally destroy the seed of the woman, pregnant with the life of God. His treason and rebellious influence caused the woman (mankind) to commit an act of spiritual adultery. This disobedient act and alliance with Satan, separated the woman from the presence of her creator, and the curse of death fell upon the eternal seed within her.

This was Satan's attempt to destroy the seed of the woman and her ability to reproduce after her kind. Now the curse of death was to invade the future of all mankind. The nature of sin was now imbedded in the heart of every child conceived.

SATAN'S JUDGMENT FORETOLD

And I will put enmity between thee and the woman (Christ), and between thy seed (Satan) and her seed (Christ); it (Christ) shall bruise thy (Satan's) head, and thou (Satan) shall bruise His (Christ's) heel. (Gen. 3:15)

This verse confirms Satan's attempt to destroy the seed of the woman. The woman represents Christ and His church. This attempt was as the bruising of Christ's heel, the end result for Satan will be the bruising of his head.

And the God of peace shall bruise Satan under your feet shortly. (Rom. 16:20)

For He must reign (Christ) till He hath put all enemies under His feet. (1Cor. 15:25)

THE FLOOD
But for Noah and his family, Satan would have succeeded in his total abortion plan.

Thank God for righteous people in the earth today, washed in the blood of the Lamb. God will always make a way of escape for the righteous.

Noah a Preacher of Righteousness
And God spared not the old world, but saved Noah the eighth person, a preacher of righteousness, bringing in the flood upon the world of the ungodly. (2Pet. 2:5)

The Lord knows how to deliver the godly out of temptations and to reserve the unjust unto the day of judgment to be punished. (2Pet. 2:9) *Many are the afflictions of the righteous: but the Lord delivers him out of them all.* (Ps. 34:19)

CORRUPTION AT CONCEPTION
In the fullness of time, or the fullness of the pregnancy period, God would present to Himself a fully matured man-child. This child is represented by a body of many members in the form of a glorious church. This church under the headship of the Lord Jesus Christ will rule and reign forever. Satan's adulterous action and rebellion, coupled with the seduction and disobedience of the woman, contaminated the holy seed and birth cycle. From the conception of mankind this corrupted seed of sin and rebellion would bring forth a deformity and premature death.

Chapter Nine

SATAN'S ABORTION PLAN   Part 2

SIN IS A TERMINAL DISEASE

There is no human remedy for those infected and born in the likeness of sinful Adam, *For as in Adam all die, even so in Christ shall all be made alive.* (1Cor. 15:22) (Rom. 5:12-21)

Satan attempted to terminate the eternal plan of God, believing for a final miscarriage or premature abortion of His child. Satan was determined that this child would not see the light of day, or the full term of the pregnancy. But light has shone in the darkness of the womb, and those that sat in darkness, the valley of the shadow of death, have seen a great light. God has not abandoned or aborted His child. He gave us the law as a temporary life support, a bandage, and a protective covering for our sin.

GOD'S REMEDY FOR SIN

Jesus Christ was God's remedy, a blood transfusion and regeneration. Jesus was God's healing injection and total cure, the ultimate victory for the obedient and believing child.

The earth is the birthing place for the Kingdom of God. Jesus is the door, the birth canal to this coming Kingdom. Only by the cleansing blood of Jesus Christ can we enter.

ONLY THE RIGHTEOUS WILL SEE THE LIGHT OF DAY

Only the righteous will endure the full nine months of the pregnancy.

Nine months on the Prophetic Calendar parallels with **6000 years** of biblical history, and **6000 years** since the conception of mankind. Only the redeemed of the Lord will come forth without a blemish or spot. Only the redeemed of the Lord will rule and reign in the seventh day of perfection, the millennial reign of Christ.

PREMATURE ABORTION OF THE WORLD

The corrupt, contaminated and unregenerate seed of mankind will be prematurely aborted and disposed of within the womb of darkness. The unbelieving soul will never see the light of His coming glorious Kingdom. Only the redeemed of the Lord and those who survive the Great Tribulation, will see His glory on earth.

Satan committed spiritual adultery with God's woman (the church) espoused to His Son; she was made by Him and for Him. This act of wickedness and rebellion was intended to destroy the eternal purpose and destiny of every child of God.

Chapter Nine

SATAN'S ABORTION PLAN   Part 3

GOD HAS NOT FORSAKEN HIS CHILDREN
Even in the womb God has not forsaken us. Even in our sin and contamination, He sent His Word to heal and deliver us in due season.

- We have a Father, we are not fatherless.
- We have a family, we are not homeless.
- We are the legitimate children of the Most High God.
- We have the eternal papers of adoption, signed and sealed in God's own blood.
- We have a place prepared for us in heaven.
- We have an inheritance that's incorruptible and never fades away.

THE ONLY WAY OUT
Satan has blinded the eyes of the unbeliever. He has given man a false sense of security in the womb of worldly darkness. (Jn. 12:40) They shall die in their sins lest they repent and never see the light of day. (Jn. 8:24) We must be born again, (Jn. 3) only the new creation in Christ will find the exit in due season. Jesus is the door (Jn. 10) to the everlasting Kingdom, the birth canal, the exit, the only way out.

I am the resurrection and the life, he that believes in Me though he were dead (in the womb of this world,) *yet shall he live.* (Jn.11: 25)

Chapter Ten

THE NIGHT IS FAR SPENT
Part 1

THE MIDNIGHT HOUR

According to The Night Watch it was high time or the midnight hour when Jesus Christ appeared on the **Prophetic Time Clock**. Paul could see that the night was far spent, and the day of the Lord was at hand.

And that, KNOWING THE TIME, that now it is high time to awake out of sleep: for now is our salvation nearer than when we believed. (Rom. 13:11)

Notice this scripture indicates we should know the time, we should be aware of His coming.

THE NIGHT IS FAR SPENT, THE DAY IS AT HAND: let us therefore cast off the works of darkness and let us put on the armor of light. (Rom. 13:12)

This verse implies The Night Watch is nearly over, as indicated on the **Prophetic Time Clock**.

See Diagram: **THE NIGHT IS FAR SPENT** - The midnight hour.

THE NIGHT IS FAR SPENT - The Midnight Hour.

Jesus Christ came in the **Midnight Hour** on the Prophetic Time Clock. The people who sat in darkness and the region of the shadow of death saw a great light. Mt. 4:16

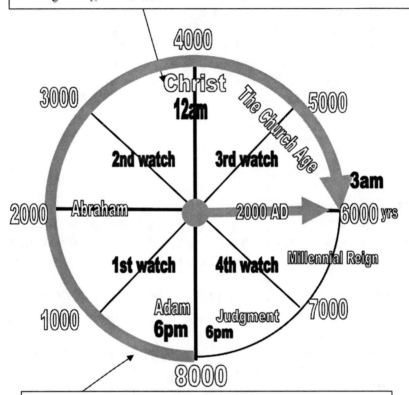

Please note! The large circled arrow represents a time frame from Adam to the closing of the Church Age, 2000-AD. This diagram reveals that three time frames of the Hebrew Night Watch have been completed; we are now entering the Fourth and Final Watch. *The night is far spent, the day is at hand.* Rom. 13:12

Chapter 10

THE NIGHT IS FAR SPENT   Part 2

DARKNESS SHALL COVER THE EARTH

We are approaching the darkest hour in world history. *Behold darkness shall cover the earth and gross darkness the people.* (Is. 60:2)

The people which sat in darkness saw great light; and to them which sat in the region and shadow of death light is sprung up. (Mt. 4:16)

SPIRITUAL DARKNESS

In God's eyes the world is sitting in spiritual darkness. The rejection of God is the rejection of light itself for all eternity. Actually, the world has been in spiritual darkness since the fall of mankind. When Adam and Eve sinned they surrendered their earthly dominion to Satan. He became the prince of this world, the prince of darkness. Through the deception of riches, lust, and the pride of life, the message of grace and forgiveness has fallen on many deaf ears. Satan has covered the earth with his cloak of maliciousness. Only the glorious light of Christ Himself can pierce the veil of darkness. Only the power of the gospel, like a two edged sword can penetrate the strongholds of the enemy camp and set the captives free.

THE PRINCE OF DARKNESS

Now is the judgment of this world: now shall the prince of this world be cast out. (Jn. 12:31)

He has blinded their eyes and hardened their heart; that they should not see with their eyes, or understand with their heart, and be converted and I should heal them. (Jn. 12:40)

Satan has actually blinded the eyes and hardened the hearts of all mankind.

For we wrestle not against flesh and blood, but against principalities, against powers, against the rulers of the darkness of this world, against spiritual wickedness in high places. (Eph. 6:12)

PUT ON THE WHOLE ARMOR OF GOD

We are involved in a spiritual battle, we need to be equipped with heaven's artillery and put on our spiritual armor to combat the forces of evil. Flesh and blood is no match for spiritual wickedness in high places. Humanity has been taken captive at Satan's will and held hostage to demonic influence.

The greatest miracle of Christianity is the opening of our spiritual eyes to see the truth. Jesus said, *"Blessed are the eyes that see what you see and the ears that hear what you hear."*

Darkness is the invasion of light, wickedness endeavoring to consume Godliness.

In the eyes of the Lord the world is in gross *thick* darkness. There is no light in a godless world; there is no light when the Light Giver has departed.

Chapter 10

THE NIGHT IS FAR SPENT   Part 3

DELIVERED FROM DARKNESS

God has delivered us from the power of darkness and translated us into the kingdom of his dear Son. (Col. 1:13) *You are a chosen generation, a royal priesthood, an holy nation, a peculiar people; that ye should show forth the praises of Him who hath called you out of darkness into his marvelous light*: (1Pet. 2:9)

We were sometimes darkness, but now we are light, walk as children of the light. Have no fellowship with the unfruitful works of darkness, but rather reprove them. Awake you that sleep and arise from the dead and Christ shall give you light. (Eph. 5:8-14)

Jesus said His Kingdom was not of this world, (Jn. 18:36) He was not of this world and we are not of this world. (Jn.17: 16) *That ye may be blameless and harmless, the sons of God, without rebuke, in the midst of a crooked and perverse nation, among whom ye shine as lights in the **world.*** (Phil. 2:15)

WATCHING AND WAITING

Let your loins be girded about, and your lights burning; and ye yourselves like unto men that wait for their lord, when he will return from the wedding; that when he cometh and knocketh, they may open unto him immediately.

Blessed are those servants whom the lord when he comes shall find watching.

And this know that if the Goodman of the house had known what hour the thief would come, he would have watched and not suffered his house to be broken through. (Lk. 12:35-39)

*Wherefore, beloved, **seeing that you look for such things,** be diligent that ye may be found of him in peace, without spot and blameless. Ye therefore, beloved, seeing **ye know these things before,** beware lest ye also, being led away with the error of the* *wicked, fall from your own steadfastness.* (2Pet. 3:14,17) The reign of darkness is nearly over. Don't look back, and don't faint in your Godly endeavor.

THE TIMES AND THE SEASONS

But of the times and the seasons, brethren, ye have no need that I write unto you. For yourselves know perfectly that the day of the lord so cometh as a thief in the night. For when they shall say, peace and safety; then sudden destruction cometh upon them, as travail upon a woman with child and they (unbelievers) shall not escape. But you, brethren, (believers) are not in darkness, that that day should overtake you as a thief.

Ye are all the children of light and the children of the day: we are not of the night, nor of darkness. Therefore let us not sleep, as do others; but let us watch and be sober. For they that sleep, sleep in the night and they that be drunken are drunken in the night. But let us, who are of the day, be sober, putting on the breastplate of faith and love and for an helmet, the hope of salvation. (1Thes. 5:1-8)

Chapter Ten

THE NIGHT IS FAR SPENT   Part 4

GOD HAS NOT APPOINTED US TO WRATH

For God hath not appointed us to wrath, but to obtain salvation by our Lord Jesus Christ, Who died for us, that, whether we wake or sleep, we should live together with him. (1Thes. 5: 9,10)

God's people should know and be aware of the approaching day of destruction. We are not appointed unto the wrath of God. We should be preparing to vacate this world, in the twinkling of an eye.

We are God's light bearers, the continuation for a season of His earthly ministry.

As darkness prevails the candle grows dim for humanity. Let us seize this day of opportunity, let us put on the Lord Jesus Christ and manifest His glorious light to a lost and dying world. We have but a fleeting moment to share this blessed hope of eternity. We are compelled by the Master to let our lights shine before men.

Possibly there shall be no other voice other than yours. *But if our gospel be hid, it is hid to them that are lost.* (2Cor. 4:3)

You are the light of the world. A city that is set on an hill cannot be hid. Neither do men light a candle, and put it under a bushel, but on a candlestick; and it gives light unto all that are in the house. Let your light so shine before men, that they may see your good works, and glorify your Father which is in heaven. (Mt. 5:14-16)

Then Jesus said unto them, *"Yet a little while is the light with you. Walk while ye have the light, lest darkness come upon you: for he that walks in darkness knows not where he goes. While you have light, believe in the light, that ye may be the children of light."* (Jn. 12:35,36)

A CROWN OF RIGHTEOUSNESS AWAITS ALL THOSE THAT LOVE HIS APPEARING (2Tim. 4:8)

Chapter Ten

THE NIGHT IS FAR SPENT   Part 5

LOVE NOT THE WORLD

Love not the world, neither the things that are in the world. If any man love the world, the love of the Father is not in him. For all that is in the world, the lust of the flesh and the lust of the eyes and the pride of life is not of the Farther, but is of the world. And the world will pass away and the lust thereof: but he that does the will of God abides for ever. (1Jn. 2:15-17)

The night is far spent, the day is at hand: let us therefore cast off the works of darkness, and let us put on the armor of light. Let us walk honestly, as in the day; not in rioting and drunkenness, not in chambering and wantonness, not in strife and envying. But put ye on the Lord Jesus Christ and make not provision for the flesh, to fulfill the lusts thereof. (Rom. 13:12-14)

That ye may be blameless and harmless, the sons of God, without rebuke, in the midst of a crooked and perverse nation, among whom ye shine as lights in the world; (Phil. 2:15)

"I am come a light into the world, that whosoever believeth on me should not abide in darkness." (Jn. 12:46)

For you were sometimes darkness, but now you are light in the Lord, walk as children of light. And have no fellowship with the unfruitful works of darkness, but rather reprove them. For it is a shame even to speak of those things which are done of them in secret. Wherefore He said, "Awake you that sleep and arise from the dead and Christ shall give you light." (Eph. 5:8-14)

This then is the message which we have heard of Him and declare unto you, that God is light, and in Him is no darkness at all. (1Jn. 1:5-7)

Chapter Eleven

THE MORNING WATCH
Part 1

THE FINAL CHAPTER
Note! In conjunction with The Night Watch it would indicate we have now entered the fourth watch and final chapter of God's plan.

- ➤ Watch No.1 Adam to Abraham **2000 years**
- ➤ Watch No.2 Abraham to Christ **2000 years**
- ➤ Watch No.3 Christ and His Church **2000 years**
- ➤ Watch No.4 **The Final Chapter 2000 years**

THE FOURTH WATCH
*"Watch you therefore: for ye know not when the master of the house comes, at evening, or at midnight, or at the cockcrowing, or in **the morning:***

Lest coming suddenly He find you sleeping.

*And what I say unto you I say unto all, **"Watch."*** (Mk. 13:33-37)

- ➤ EVENING WATCH **6pm till 9pm**
- ➤ MIDNIGHT WATCH **9pm till 12am**
- ➤ COCK CROWING **12am till 3am**
- ➤ MORNING WATCH **3am till 6am**

THE BRIGHT AND MORNING STAR

The morning watch is breaking forth with flickers of His glorious light shimmering on the horizon. The Bright and Morning Star is about to arise with healing in His wings and catch away the remnant of the church age. He has waited long for the precious fruit of the earth. Christ will soon thrust in His sickle and reap the tender sweet grapes of His beloved bride. The marriage supper of the Lamb is being prepared and the invitations are out, *"make yourself ready church, the hour is upon us"*.

A GENERATION OF PASSIONATE BELIEVERS

The morning watch is ushering in a generation of passionate believers, true worshipers devoted to HOLINESS and the upward call of Christ.

This generation is being observed by a great cloud of heavenly witnesses, (Heb. 12:1) cheering them on for the final quarter of God's redemption plan.

The church age is handing us the baton for the last leg of the race. Run to win, run for the prize possession of Christ Himself. Don't look back; set your sites on Jesus and press toward the mark of the high calling of God.

Finish the race set before you and receive your crown of glory. Be encouraged and fight the good fight, it's time to lift up your hands and strengthen those feeble knees.

Seize this glorious day and claim your inheritance. Rise up and be counted. This is the day the prophets desired to see and rejoiced!

Chapter Eleven

THE MORNING WATCH   Part 2

THE GATHERING DISPENSATION

I truly believe we have entered the GATHERING dispensation of all things in Christ. (Eph. 1:10)

God is gathering His people for the final exploit of the Promised Land.

It's harvest time saints, and God is preparing to reap the long awaited fruit of His vineyard, and gather the wheat into His storehouse.

Judgment has begun in the house of the Lord. God is shaking and sifting wickedness from the household of faith, severing unbelief and compromise from His glorious church.

("Oh Lord, refine me and burn away the chaff of unbelief and disobedience. Remove the choking weeds, the cares of this life. Scatter the little foxes that spoil the vine and receive my tender fruit. I am separated unto you, I will not touch the unclean thing, I will keep my garment unspotted for your glorious appearing.")

The most exciting aspect for me concerning this revelation is the morning watch. The morning watch represents the beginning of the seventh day, **7000 years** from Adam and creation. According to biblical history, we are entering the dawning of the seventh day, the closing of **6000 years** since creation, and the dawning of the seventh millennium. That puts us (the church) at the changing of the guard, the beginning of the morning watch, **2000-AD.**

Six is the number of man, I truly believe the devil's lease is up on planet earth, Satan is about to be evicted, and replaced by the King of Kings and Lord of Lords.

THE FINAL FULFILLMENTS

The Fourth Watch or Morning Watch is dedicated to Jesus Christ and His glorious church.

God will be glorified on earth in the sight of mortal men; the riches of the Gentiles are stored up for the righteous and the Kingdom of God.

The Fourth Watch incorporates:

> ➤ The Final Harvest
> ➤ The gathering of His glorious church
> ➤ The upward call or rapture of the saints unto Him
> ➤ The marriage supper of the Lamb
> ➤ The second coming of Christ and judgment on the antichrist system
> ➤ The millennial reign of Christ on earth
> ➤ The Great White Throne of judgment (The second death)
> ➤ The new beginning

THE FINAL TWO DAYS ARE NOW BEING DETERMINED UPON THE EARTH!

DAY SEVEN:(The great day of the Lord)

The seventh day incorporates His judgment on the world antichrist system. The rapture and resurection of the saints. The marriage supper of the Lamb and His glorious millennial reign on earth.

DAY EIGHT: (The Final Judgment)

At the closing of the millennial reign of Christ, Satan is loosed from the pit for a short season. He makes war against Christ and His saints; God consumes Satan and his adversaries with fire from heaven. The Great White Throne appears and judgment begins for the spiritually dead, this is the second death. The first death is physical death; the second death is spiritual death, the lake of fire and eternal separation from God. (Rev. 20)

THE CYCLE OF REDEMPTION
Eight days (8000 years) completes the cycle of REDEMPTION on the **Prophetic Time Clock**.

THE CYCLE OF PURIFICATION
Eight days completes the **cycle of purification**, the final cleansng by fire of the Temple of God.
God has purified a people unto Himself. (Tit. 2:14)

DIVINE JUDGMENT IS NOW COMPLETE, AND BEHOLD, HE MAKES ALL THINGS NEW!

Chapter Twelve

THE END OF ALL THINGS
Part 1

THE END OF THE WORLD

God has set a time for this world system to end, making way for a new beginning on planet earth, the establishment of the Kingdom of God. The 20th century church is witnessing the culmination of all things, as the Apostle Paul said, *these things are written for our admonition, upon whom the ENDS OF THE WORLD ARE COME.* (1Cor. 10:11)

According to The Night Watch, end time harvest began with the appearance of Jesus Christ on the Prophetic Calendar.

The following scriptures are added to confirm that man in his mortal state, does have an end: Flesh and blood cannot inherit the Kingdom of God, this mortal body of flesh and blood must put on immortality. (1Cor. 15: 50-53)

The end of all things is at hand, be sober and watch unto prayer. (1Pet. 4:7)

And as Jesus sat upon the Mount of Olives, the disciples came unto him privately, saying, "Tell us, when shall these things be? and what shall be the sign of thy coming, and of the end of the world?" (Mt. 24:3)

He that shall endure unto the end, the same shall be saved. And this gospel of the kingdom shall be preached in all the world for a witness unto all nations; and then shall the end come. (Mt. 24:13-14)

But now once in the end of the world he (Christ*) has appeared to put away sin by the sacrifice of himself.* (Heb. 9:26)

The harvest is the end of the world; and the reapers are the angels. (Mt. 13:39)

God has in these last days spoken unto us by his Son, whom he has appointed heir of all things, by whom also he made the worlds. (Heb. 1:1,2) *God shall also confirm you unto the end that ye may be blameless in the day of our Lord Jesus Christ.*(1Cor. 1:8) *It is appointed unto men once to die, but after this the judgment.* (Heb. 9:27) *For we are made partakers of Christ, if we hold the beginning of our confidence steadfast unto the end.* (Heb. 3:14)

Jesus spoke unto them, saying, "All power is given unto me in heaven and in earth. Go you therefore and teach all nations, baptizing them in the name of the Father and of the Son and of the Holy Ghost: Teaching them to observe all things what ever I have commanded you and lo, I am with you always, even unto the end of the world." (Mt. 28:18-20)

"I am Alpha and Omega, the beginning and the ending, says the Lord, "which is and which was and which is to come, the Almighty." (Rev. 1:8)

Chapter Twelve

THE END OF ALL THINGS   Part 2

BEHOLD! HE MAKES ALL THINGS NEW

These scriptures have been added to establish the biblical fact that there is a definite end to this world's system. If that fact is not established in the hearts and minds of humanity, the false sense of security, comfort and the pride of life, will be a **fatal attraction**.

GOD HAS NO BEGINNING OR END

The biblical phrases such as Alfa and Omega, Beginning and End, First and Last are words descriptive of this world only.

Scripture teaches us that God has no end or beginning, He is forever, HE IS EVERLASTING.

The Bible is God's revelation of Himself to mankind. The Bible is God's attempt to redeem fallen man, by suffering Himself personally, through the cross of Jesus Christ.

IN THE END GOD WILL DESTROY

The Lord is not slack concerning his promise, as some men count slackness; but is longsuffering to us-ward, not willing that any should perish, but that all should come to repentance.

But the day of the Lord will come as a thief in the night; in the which the heavens shall pass away with a great noise and the elements shall melt with fervent heat, the earth also and the works that are therein shall be burned up. Seeing then that all these things shall be dissolved, what manner of persons ought ye to be in all holy conversation and godliness,

Looking for and hasting unto the coming of the day of God, wherein the heavens being on fire shall be dissolved and the elements shall melt with fervent heat?

Nevertheless we, according to his promise, look for new heavens and a new earth, wherein dwells righteousness (2Pet. 3:9-13).

BEHOLD! HE MAKES ALL THINGS NEW

And I saw a new heaven and a new earth: for the first heaven and the first earth were passed away; and there was no more sea. And I John saw the holy city, the new Jerusalem, coming down from God out of heaven, prepared as a bride adorned for her husband.

And I heard a great voice out of heaven saying, "Behold, the tabernacle of God is with men and he will dwell with them and they shall be his people and God himself shall be with them and be their God.

And God shall wipe away all tears from their eyes; and there shall be no more death, neither sorrow, nor crying, neither shall there be any more pain: for the former things are passed away.

And he that sat upon the throne said, "Behold, I make all things new." And he said unto me, "Write, for these words are true and faithful." (Rev. 21:1-5)

Thank God there is something better to look forward to than this present world of turmoil, greed and wickedness. According to The Night Watch, darkness is nearly over for those who love God, and a new day is on the horizon.

"IF YOUR DESIRE IS FOR GOOD AND NOT EVIL, WHY NOT ACCEPT GOD'S WONDERFUL PLAN OF SALVATION AND EVERLASTING LOVE FOR YOU?"

THE BEGINNING

CONCLUSION

I pray this revelation will stir your heart concerning this urgent hour in church history. Perilous times are forecasted and men's hearts will fail them for fear concerning worldly events.

It's time to press into God like never before. He will show Himself strong on behalf of His faithful children. God will be glorified in His people and sustain them with **peace, protection and provision.**

We must know Him in a personal and intimate way this side of heaven. We must become familiar with His voice and walk in His perfect will, redeeming the time.

Don't be left behind in the potter's kiln of God's purification beyond the prescribed time. We must be fired to perfection in the furnace of His love. We must be ready to depart, taken out before the temperature rises in Judgment. Nothing that is defiled will endure the refiners fire.

Don't be left behind in the womb of darkness beyond the **ninth month** of pregnancy. The Kingdom of God is about to be birthed in the earth. Those remaining in the womb will be aborted and perish, due to their rejection of Jesus Christ and the grace of God.

I believe this revelation is a warning from God, a cry in the night to awaken all believers. This book confirms the conviction of many today that are sensing by the Holy Spirit, the imminent return of Christ. Get ready for departure, pack your spiritual suitcase, trim your lamp, and make your pathway straight. Your eternal destiny is in the balance and a firm commitment to the Lord Jesus Christ is required. **Today is the day of Salvation.** (2Cor. 6:2)

PRAYER

PRAYER OF SALVATION

Jesus, forgive me, I turn to You and confess my sin; I repent for my disobedience and unbelief.

I receive you now as my personal Savior and friend; I now declare before the world, that Jesus is Lord, the Son of the Living God! Amen. (Romans. 10:9,10)

Having prayed this prayer of Salvation, I believe by faith I am saved!

Date: _____ Sign: _____

PERSONAL PRAYER

Jesus, make me ready for Your return. Lead me through the waters of baptism and fill me with Your Holy Spirit. Help me to read my Bible daily and share my faith with others. Lead me to a place where I can fellowship and worship with my new family in Christ, Amen.

CONTACT

For further information and contact go to:

Website: www.roymills.com email: info@roymills.com

LaVergne, TN USA
22 March 2010
176837LV00001B/12/P